Wear Whatever!

Story by Janeen Brian
Illustrations by Bece Luna

Wear Whatever!

Text: Janeen Brian
Publishers: Tania Mazzeo and Eliza Webb
Series consultant: Amanda Sutera
Hands on Heads Consulting
Editor: Jess Mackay
Project editor: Annabel Smith
Designer: Jess Kelly
Project designer: Danielle Maccarone
Illustrations: Bece Luna
Production controller: Renee Tome

NovaStar

ISBN 978 0 17 033488 4

Cengage Learning Australia
Level 5, 80 Dorcas Street
Southbank VIC 3006 Australia
Phone: 1300 790 853
Email: aust.nelsonprimary@cengage.com

For learning solutions, visit **cengage.com.au**

Printed in China by 1010 Printing International Ltd
1 2 3 4 5 6 7 29 28 27 26 25

Nelson acknowledges the Traditional Owners and Custodians of the lands of all First Nations Peoples. We pay respect to Elders past and present, and extend that respect to all First Nations Peoples today.

Contents

Chapter 1

Caught Out

At the sound of the footsteps in the hall, Archie froze. Who was it? He was still holding the zip on the dress.

His mum was running the coffee machine and singing in the kitchen. So it had to be Daisy! Why had his big sister come home so early from netball?

Archie panicked. “Come on! Come on!” he muttered. His fingers trembled. His palms grew clammy. He wriggled the zip, but it was stuck. Archie glanced at the door. He had to get the dress off!

The door swung open. Twelve-year-old Archie and his sister gaped at each other.

Daisy shut the door behind her and said, “Why are you in my room, Arch? And why are you wearing my dress?”

The words stuck in Archie's throat. Then he stammered, "I didn't expect you home so –"

"Early," finished Daisy. "I can see that." Sitting down on the end of her bed, she said, "But why have you got my dress on? It's not a dress-up costume, Arch."

"I know that. It's just ..."

Daisy raised her eyebrows, waiting for a response from her younger brother.

Archie reached for the zip again, then let his hands fall to his sides. "You won't laugh?"

Daisy shook her head.

"Or tell Mum?"

"Promise."

"It's because I like the feel of it," said Archie sheepishly. He bit his lip. "Daisy, can you just help me get out of it? There's something wrong with the zip. I'm sorry."

Daisy jiggled the zip till it slid free. "So, you've put the dress on before, then?"

"Yeah," Archie said in a quiet voice. "And others. But I like this one best." He smoothed the blue fabric of the skirt.

"That's cos the colour suits you," said Daisy. She tilted her head. "But it's too big. Needs a belt. Wait there."

To Archie's astonishment, Daisy darted towards her wardrobe.

Then something, or someone, caught his eye in the window. In a flash he saw it was his two mates, Dillon and Gael. The two boys stood and stared, with their mouths open like fish.

Archie's face flushed red.

"Here, try on this belt, Arch," Daisy began.

"Get this off me, please, Daisy! Quick!"

"Why, what's ..." she began, but was interrupted by a knock on the door.

Their mum opened the door just as Archie was whipping the dress over his head. "Arch," said his mum, "Dillon and Gael are –" She stopped. She looked first at Daisy and then back at Archie. Archie tossed the dress onto the bed and ran his fingers through his hair.

"Hi, Mum," he croaked.

"Your friends are here," said Mum in an even voice. Then she turned her head. "Boys, Arch is in there. Go in."

Chapter 2

An Awkward Game

"Welcome, one and all," said Daisy, hanging up the belt in the wardrobe. "Hi, Dillon. Hi, Gael."

"Hi," the boys chorused.

"Hey." Archie pulled at his t-shirt and slid his hands into the pockets of his jeans.

The dress lay rumpled on the bed. Archie glanced at it, his heart thumping.

"Nice dress," said Dillon, as Daisy took it to put away.

Dillon's words hung pointedly in the air. An awkward silence filled the room.

"Thanks," said Daisy. "I've got some matching nail polish, Dillon, if you want to try some."

Dillon scoffed. "As if!"

"Lots of cool football players and singers wear nail polish," said Daisy, standing alongside Archie. "So why not?"

“Because I’m not a girl,” said Dillon. “And I don’t wear dresses.” He shot a glance at Archie.

“And yet I wear caps and track pants even though some people might consider them to be boys’ clothes,” said Daisy, with a pretend puzzled look on her face.

Gael broke in, “Hey, Arch. Do you want to go skateboarding? Or have a kick?” He spun a football in his hand.

“Yeah, don’t let me hold you up.” Daisy grinned, opening the door. She gave Archie a friendly squeeze of his arm as he walked out with the others.

“Just going to the park, Mum,” Archie called as the three boys passed by the kitchen. His mum was at the table, her laptop open.

“See you later, Arch.” She waved to them all.

Archie breathed a sigh of relief that his mum hadn’t mentioned the dress. But he felt like it shouldn’t have come as a surprise to her. Clothes had always interested him for as long as he could remember.

Way back, his mum used to buy fancy-dress costumes from charity shops. Archie was always fascinated by the different colours and textures.

Of all his kindergarten friends, including Gael and Dillon, it was always Archie and his friend Gloria who loved wearing them. The two of them would play dress-ups all the time.

Gael bounced the ball all the way to the park, except when Dillon tried to grab it. Archie pretended to laugh. But even at the park, his heart wasn't in the game. Dillon caught him out more than once, missing a catch or fumbling a handball.

"You going to tell us about the dress, Arch?" Dillon finally said. "Cos you wouldn't be able to play footy in a dress!"

"Leave it, Dillon," said Gael.

"Just want to know why," said Dillon.

"It was nothing," Archie mumbled. He couldn't tell them, even though they were his mates. The words wouldn't come out right.

"I know why!" Dillon punched the air. "All this study we're doing at school about clothing history and culture! It's gone to your head, hasn't it?"

Dillon gave Archie a playful punch on his arm. Gael gave a faint smile.

"Could be," said Archie, going along with it.

A few minutes later, Archie decided to head home. As he left the park, he could hear Dillon and Gael whispering.

It had nothing to do with their school project on clothing, and he had a feeling Dillon suspected that, too. But what would happen now? Would Dillon and Gael still want to be his mates?

Archie kicked at a stone on his way home. His thoughts swung from being caught out wearing a dress, to the school Wear Whatever Day where kids could wear whatever they liked. It was on the last day of term, only two weeks away. Gloria and a few other kids had organised a disco in the school hall that day as well. He'd been looking forward to it. Mucking about with Dillon, Gael and Gloria would've been great fun. But now he wasn't so sure.

Archie's uncertain feelings didn't change during the next few days because Gael and Dillon kept their distance. At school, they often headed to the oval without him, or gave half-hearted waves. Sometimes Archie and Gloria played handball with them. But it wasn't the same.

Gloria noticed. Later that week, when she and Archie were at the drinking fountains, she asked, "What's up with you three?"

"Nothing," he said.

Gloria gave him a steely look. "You're not good at telling lies, Arch. What's going on?"

Archie wiped his mouth and looked down. Then, almost in one breath, he told Gloria the whole story of the boys catching him wearing Daisy's dress.

"Is that a crime?" said Gloria with a toss of her hair. "That's what our projects are all about, aren't they? Researching different clothes for different people. Gael's family comes from Scotland. And Dillon's family lived in lots of countries before coming here."

"It's more that ... I wasn't just dressing up, Gloria. I like wearing dresses. Not out, or anything. It's just the feel of them."

Gloria shrugged. "I like you whatever you wear, Arch."

"Thanks." He smiled, but maybe he'd lost two other friends.

Chapter 3

The Boy in the Book

It was in the library that afternoon when Archie saw the photo of another boy wearing a dress.

It'd come as a shock and a surprise at the same time.

Their teacher, Miss Quigley, had given the class a chance to complete their projects on clothing history and culture. The kids had all dashed to find a seat at a table.

Gael had beckoned to Archie, which gave him a warm feeling. But Dillon sat at another table.

Archie finished his project and picked up a book. He'd only turned over a few pages, when he came to an old-fashioned photo of a boy in a frilly white dress. The information stated that in the 1800s, boys wore dresses until they were about five or six years old.

Archie gawped.

Dillon happened to be walking past and saw the photo. “Give it a rest, Archie. Not more boys in dresses.”

A few kids nearby heard and glanced up, expectantly.

“Project work,” said Archie.

Dillon grunted and walked on, but it left Archie with an unsettled feeling in his stomach.

That night, at the kitchen table, Daisy said, “It’s a no-brainer. You’ve got to face up to Dillon and Gael. Tell them you like wearing dresses. Don’t beat around the bush any more.”

“But what if they ditch me as a mate?” Archie’s voice was strained.

Daisy shrugged, but in a kind way. “Then that’s up to them, Arch. Sorry, but it is.”

“What’s going on?” Their mum walked up to the table carrying a dish of vegetable lasagne.

Daisy looked at Archie and gestured towards their mum. “Tell her.”

Mum pulled out a chair and sat down. “I’m listening,” she said.

Archie pressed his lips together, then took a deep breath and blurted everything out.

For a while, no one spoke. Only the sounds of a few birds chirping crept in through the open window.

Archie had his elbows on the table, his head sunk low in his cupped hands.

“So,” Mum said finally. “You’ve been trying on Daisy’s dresses.”

Archie nodded.

“And Dillon and Gael saw you and have been making things a bit tough.”

“Mainly Dillon,” said Archie. He wasn’t sure what Gael thought.

“Well, you know what, love?” said Mum, taking his hand. “You always liked dressing up and choosing your own outfits each day, ever since you were little. It’s part of who you are. And tomorrow after school we’re going shopping. You and me. And we’re going to buy you a dress that fits.”

Archie raised his head. A warm wetness filled his eyes.

“Thanks, Mum.” He leapt up and hugged her.

"See, Arch!" cried Daisy. She grabbed Archie's cheeks and squeezed them. "You just have to speak up."

Archie smiled and hugged his sister.

"And make sure you get some matching nail polish while you're there!" Daisy added.

Chapter 4

Try It On

It was like a different world.

The following afternoon, Archie wandered into the department store. He followed Mum past the boys' clothing racks and displays to another section altogether.

"No rush, Arch," Mum said. She wandered about, shifting dresses and tops along on their coat hangers.

Archie took his time, looking at this dress and that, taking in the colours and fabrics. The feel of each one. For a while everything felt strange, as if he was in the wrong area. As though at any minute, he would be whisked back to the boys' department. But as time passed and no such thing happened, he relaxed until he found the right dress. It was green with gathered layers and short sleeves.

He lifted the coat hanger and looked about for Mum.

"Mum," he said, walking up to her. "I like this one."

Mum took the dress and turned it around.

"So do I, Arch," Mum replied.

"Can we get it?" said Archie.

"Yeah, love. But we have to see if it's the right size. Ah!" she said and pointed. "The fitting rooms are over there."

Archie paled. "Can't we just take it home? Try it on there?"

"If it's the wrong size, Arch, we'll have to come all the way back and get another one. Best we do it now. Come on."

Edging a little behind Mum, Archie walked up to the fitting rooms.

"Just the one?" said the woman behind the counter. She looked at the dress and gave Archie's mum a smile.

Inside the fitting rooms, Archie pulled open the curtain of an empty cubicle and took the dress from Mum. He hung it on a hook and turned.

"Mum, can you please wait outside?"

"Sure, Archie," she said.

Archie drew the curtain across.

A short time later, he parted it and peeked out. "You can come in now."

Mum stepped inside. The long mirrors reflected Archie in the green dress, showing all angles.

"How does it feel, Arch?" she said with a shaky smile.

"It feels good, Mum," he said. "What do you think?"

"I think it looks lovely."

Once the dress had been paid for, the pair set off towards the beauty department. Archie carried the bag with the dress and occasionally glanced down. His heart thumped each time he saw the soft green shape tucked inside.

"Wow!" he said, as he scanned the wide range of coloured nail polishes. "So many!"

"Every colour of the rainbow," said Mum.

"This green one, I think," said Archie.

"Matches the dress exactly," said Mum. Then to the assistant she said, "We'll have this, thanks."

"Lovely colour," he said. "Very popular with the girls at the moment."

Archie's cheeks flushed, but his embarrassment disappeared when Mum handed him the paper bag and said, "All yours, love."

The assistant turned to Archie and smiled warmly.

As they drove home, Archie clutched both bags. It was like a dream.

For that whole afternoon, he'd forgotten about everything else: the hassle and confusion with his mates, school and even Wear Whatever Day, which was only a few days away.

At a traffic light, Archie said, "Mum?"

"Mmm," she said, her eyes fixed on the traffic signal.

"Thanks for everything. You're the best."

The light flicked to green, and Mum pressed down on the accelerator. "You're welcome, my love."

Archie wished he had a camera for the moment Daisy saw the dress later that day. Her face lit up like a firecracker.

"It's fabulous, Arch! Wish it was in my size!"

Archie laughed.

"Show me. Put it on."

Archie couldn't wait to put the dress back on. When he was ready, Daisy nodded. "Even better on," she said. "I wish your friends could see you in it."

Archie paused. An idea suddenly zapped into his head.

"I'm going to wear it to Wear Whatever Day," he said. "There's a disco as well."

Daisy's expression faltered. "You're wearing it out?" she said. "To school?"

Archie's courage quivered.

"Everyone else will be wearing whatever they want," he said.

"Yeah!" Daisy's tone lifted. "And my brother will be wearing what he wants – a green dress!"

"And green nail polish," said Archie, feeling brighter.

"Whoo-woo!"

Chapter 5

The Fight

Archie heard the loud shouts as he approached the classroom the next morning. A group of kids jostled and huddled around a couple of others, who were scuffling and yelling. Archie hurried when he saw that Dillon was one of those fighting.

"Dillon!" cried Gael, ducking blows while pulling at his arm. "Forget it! Come on!"

Dillon yanked free and glared at Archie. Elbowing his way out of the tussle, Dillon stormed off with Gael following. The other kids parted, mumbling to each other.

Archie caught up. "Hey, Dillon," he said. "Are you okay? What happened? What's wrong?"

Dillon stopped and leaned in closer. "You!" he snapped.

Archie straightened, taken aback. "Me? What've I done?"

"Kids are talking about you, Arch! About why you were interested in that boy in the history book. The boy wearing a dress."

"To be fair, Dillon," Gael broke in, "you said something about it in the library. Frankie overheard you. So then you blabbed that we'd seen Arch wearing a dress and –"

"Now they're making fun of Gael and me," snapped Dillon. "Frankie wants to know why we'd want to be friends with a boy who wears dresses."

Archie felt sick.

Dillon's face creased with anger. His cheeks glowed red. He was about to walk away from them both, but Gael held him back.

"Wait," he said. Turning to Archie, he said, "Arch. You've got to tell us what's going on. We're your friends and –"

Dillon made a noise in his throat.

Gael ignored it and went on. "What's with this dress wearing? Is it dress-up stuff or ...?"

Archie knew the time had come. This was the moment he'd dreaded. And yet it had felt worse not to have been able to share it with Dillon and Gael. Archie knew in his heart that what Daisy said was true. If it broke the friendship, then there was nothing he could do about it. He had to take the risk.

"Okay," he said. "I'll tell you."

Dillon leaned against the wall and crossed his arms, but Gael looked Archie in the eye, waiting.

"I've always liked dressing up," Archie said. "You know that. But then, one day, I saw Daisy wearing a blue silk dress. It looked really nice on her. And something happened. I wanted to try it on too. So I did. But only when no one was around," he added.

He paused. Dillon was looking at the ground.

"Go on," said Gael.

"I don't know. It just felt good. I only put it on for a short time. But then, I'd go back when Daisy was out and try on others. It's just something ... I can't explain. I just like wearing dresses."

Archie paused. "But I didn't know what to say to people. Not to you two, not to Mum or Daisy.

I was embarrassed. I didn't know any other boy who liked wearing dresses. So I couldn't talk to anyone." By now his voice had become so soft he hardly heard it himself.

Kids ran past them, laughing, throwing balls or calling out to others.

Dillon looked up but stared past Archie, towards the oval.

"So, Arch," said Gael, "do you think you'll always want to wear them?" Archie heard the hesitation and concern in his voice.

He knew he had to tell the truth. Even Gloria had said he wasn't much good at lying. But the truth was, he didn't know.

He shrugged.

"Do you think," Gael continued, picking at his words like a bird pecking for the best worm, "that you might want to be ... a girl?"

Gael's words caused a rushing sound in Archie's ears, and they echoed for what seemed like a long time.

The question bowled him over. But again, he shook his head. "I don't know. I don't think so, but I don't know."

At that moment, the school bell rang, and the sound shattered the conversation. In silence, the boys strode to their classroom.

At the end of school, Archie hardly knew what lessons he'd done.

Chapter 6

Wear Whatever Day

Back home, he got himself a drink of water, went to his room and shut the door.

"Archie?" called Mum.

"Be out later," called back.

For a while, he lay on his bed, thinking about the day. The fight. Knowing that he was the cause of it. The questions that turned him inside out, and all the other things that needed sorting. One of them was what he was going to wear to school tomorrow. Because it was Friday, the last day of term.

Wear Whatever Day.

After dinner, Archie returned to his room, took the green dress from the wardrobe and hung it on the doorknob. His thoughts flew back to the wonderful afternoon when he and his mum had bought the dress. Filled with the memory, he sat down to paint his nails.

But, as Archie waited for them to dry, he remembered all that had happened since then. His stomach churned. That night, he couldn't sleep. From time to time, he woke up and found himself twisted up in the sheets.

When morning came, he rubbed his eyes blearily and slowly got dressed.

As he walked into the kitchen, Daisy took one look at him and burst out laughing. “What’ve you got on?”

“Clothes,” said Archie.

“Yes,” said Daisy, putting her piece of toast back on the plate. “And what does the calendar say, Arch? It says it’s Friday, the last day of term. Wear Whatever Day. Ring any bells?”

Archie didn’t smile. “I’m wearing this,” he said and shook cereal into his bowl.

"Wait! What?" cried Daisy. "You have that great dress, your nails are glossy green and you say you're wearing jeans and a t-shirt?"

"Yep." Archie slurped at his cereal, not caring if he sounded like a dog gulping water.

"Morning all," said Mum. "Anyone put the kettle on yet? No? I guess I'll –" She stopped. "Archie?"

"I've already said something, Mum," said Daisy. "He knows what day it is."

"What's going on?" Mum moved towards his chair. "I thought you were going to wear ..."

Archie stood, pushed his chair in with a noisy clatter and grabbed his school bag. "Well, I'm not. See ya."

Daisy jumped to her feet and took hold of Archie's shoulders. "You're not going anywhere," she said in a firm voice. "Not till you tell us what's happened."

"Sit, Arch," said Mum. "You've got to tell us. You can't bury things like this. Maybe we can help."

"You can't."

"Try us," said Daisy, pulling out his chair.

Archie slumped down and dropped his bag at his feet.

"There was a fight," he began. And then he told them the rest of what'd happened and what Gael had asked him.

"And I don't know the answers. I don't." Archie lowered his head. "I don't think I can wear the dress today."

"Because of Dillon and Gael?" said Mum.

"Yeah, mainly."

"They're your friends, Arch, but friendships change," Mum continued. "They're finding it hard to understand, that's all."

"So am I, Mum."

"I know. But give yourself time, love. All of you."

The next minute, Daisy had a grip on Archie's shoulders and was marching him into his room. "You've got five minutes to change, Arch, because I'm walking with you to school."

Chapter 7

Keep Your Head Up

Daisy tilted her head approvingly. "That's better!" she said. "It fits you well, Arch. No need for a belt, eh?"

Together they waved goodbye to their mum and set off on the short distance to the school. The breeze whisked the dress about Archie's legs.

"Keep your head up," Daisy said repeatedly. At the gate, she added, "I won't give you a bear hug. Too many people watching. But have fun, little brother. And remember, keep your –"

"Okay, Daisy," Archie couldn't help himself from grinning. "I know the rest."

From the school hall came strains of music. Gloria and the rest of the class disco group had put a lot of time into planning this. It would be two full hours, with no school assembly beforehand.

The hall was right in front of him, but Archie suddenly struggled to get his feet to move. Some kids were giving him sideways glances. Others were staring. Others called out, “Hey, Archie!” just as they would on any other day.

But it was as he reached the doorway that his legs buckled. His mouth went dry. It was too much. He couldn’t do it after all. Wearing a dress for real, not as a dress-up, not in the privacy of his own home, was a big ask. He was about to turn around when a voice stopped him.

"Archie! Come in!" The hall was dim. But when Gloria stepped closer, Archie cried out in astonishment. Gloria's eyes sparkled and they both burst out laughing.

She was wearing the exact same green dress!

"That's hilarious!" She gasped, her hand to her chest. "We both have good taste."

A couple of kids had now noticed the dresses and were joining in the fun and telling others. But Archie's eyes were searching for two particular kids in the crowd.

"I'm just going to check the playlist, Arch," said Gloria.

"Okay," he said absentmindedly. His mates were nowhere to be seen. Was that his answer then? Had his friends decided to stay away because they guessed he might wear a dress?

"Hey, Arch!" It was Gael's voice. Where was he?

"Over here!"

Archie walked towards the corner of the stage and there was Gael. And Dillon. Gael was dressed in a kilt, a Scottish skirt, and Dillon wore a dark blue kaftan that flowed to his feet. Archie stared at them in surprise.

"Hey, Arch," said Dillon. "Gael and me thought we could all hang out together." He paused and gave an awkward grin. "Sorry about earlier. I didn't know what to … I couldn't …"

"It's okay," said Archie. He didn't know whether to laugh or cry. His mates were here. Dressed in those clothes. "Look at you!" he cried. "Look at you!"

With that, the music blared louder.

"Dance, everyone!" shouted Gloria. "Dance!"

And they did.